>Contents

Me and my fire engine   **6**

In the cab   **8**

Fire engine power   **10**

Ladders and lights   **12**

The pump and hoses   **14**

More equipment   **16**

Emergency!   **18**

At the fire   **20**

Tidying up   **22**

More fire engines   **24**

Be a fire engine driver   **26**

Fire engine parts   **28**

Word bank   **29**

Index   **30**

Me and my fire engine

Hello! This mega machine is a fire engine. I am a fire engine driver.

fir ne

... is my fire
engine

Written by Chris Oxlade
Photography by Andy Crawford

First published in 2006 by
Franklin Watts
338 Euston Road
London NW1 3BH

Franklin Watts Australia
45-51 Huntley Street, Alexandria
NSW 2015

Editor: Jennifer Schofield
Designer: Jemima Lumley
Photography: Andy Crawford
Fire engine driver: Suzanne Hastings

The Publisher would like to thank Manners PR, Suzanne Hastings, Station Commander
Tony New and all at Bedfordshire and Luton Fire
and Rescue Services for their help in producing this book.

A CIP catalogue record for this book
is available from the British Library.

ISBN: 978 0 7496 6538 8
Dewey Classification: 629'225

Printed in China

Franklin Watts is a division of
Hachette Children's Books

▽ *A fire engine helps to fight fires and rescue people.*

> In the cab

The front part of the fire engine is called the cab.

▲ *To drive the fire engine I sit in the cab. I use a steering wheel, levers and pedals.*

> *I use the radio to talk to the fire station.*

radio

∨ *There are seats for other firefighters behind me.*

Fire engine power

The fire engine's parts are worked by an engine.

< *The engine is under the cab.*

> *To see the engine, the cab needs to be lifted up.*

> The engine turns the wheels.

< The tyres are chunky for driving over rough ground.

Ladders and lights

There is equipment on
my fire engine's roof.

> *Firefighters use these ladders to climb into buildings.*

∨ *Flashing lights and loud sirens warn people that the fire engine is coming.*

> The pump and hoses

At the back of the fire engine are a water pump and hoses.

> *The water pump pushes water along hoses to the fire.*

14

▼ The hoses are kept in lockers.
They are rolled up and ready to use.

More equipment

There is a lot more equipment inside the fire engine's lockers.

> *Firefighters use this tool to cut open crashed cars.*

< *This fan is called a PPV unit. It is used to get rid of smoke after a fire.*

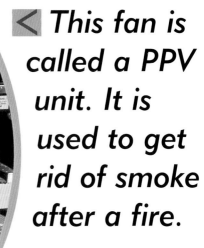

Emergency!

When there is an emergency
I rush to the fire engine.

I need to drive to the fire quickly.

< *I switch on the lights and sirens to warn other drivers.*

At the fire

We have arrived at a
building that is on fire.

△ *I must change into my
firefighter's clothes now.*

We quickly get the
equipment we need
to fight the fire.

> Tidying up

We have put the fire out.
It is time to tidy up.

∧ *We roll up the hoses and put the equipment back in its lockers.*

▼ *Now it is time to drive back to the fire station.*

> More fire engines

These are some of the other types of fire engines that we use.

∧ *This fire engine has a platform that reaches high into the air.*

Not all emergencies are on land. Sometimes we have to go out onto lakes, rivers and seas.

∧ *This is a fire rescue boat. It is used when there is an emergency on water.*

Be a fire engine driver

You need to learn a lot before you can drive the fire engine.

V You need to know the different parts of the fire engine.

∧ You need to practise climbing up ladders.

⋀ **You need to learn about your fireproof clothes.**

⋀ ▷ **You need to know how to use all the equipment.**

> Fire engine parts

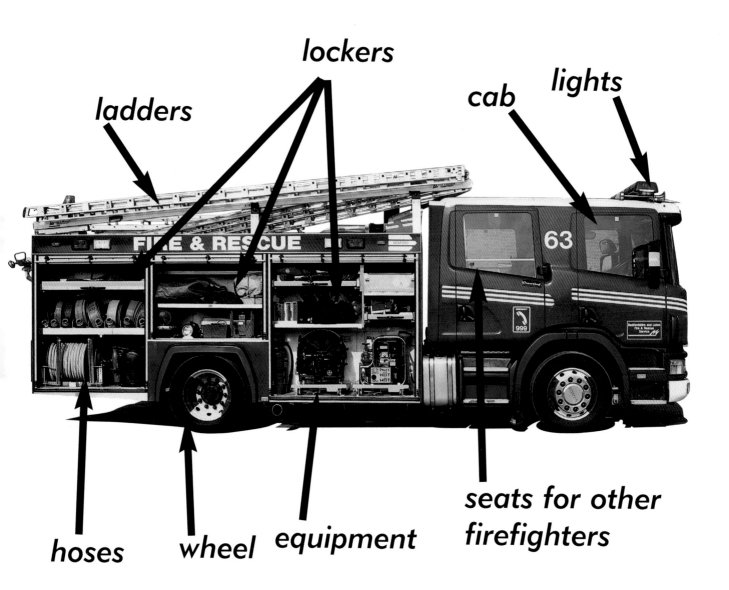

lockers

lights

cab

ladders

FIRE & RESCUE

63

seats for other firefighters

hoses

wheel

equipment

▷ **Word bank**

emergency – when firefighters have to put out a fire

equipment – the machines and tools that firefighters use at emergencies

fireproof – something that fire cannot burn

lockers – the place on the fire engine where firefighters' equipment is kept

radio – the machine used to talk to the fire station when firefighters are in the fire engine

rescue – to help someone out of the place that is on fire

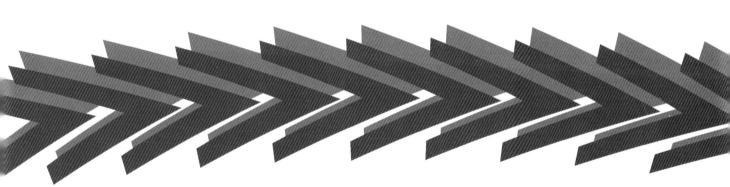

Websites

Firefighters help thousands of people every year. To find out more about their jobs and the work that they do, log on to www.fire.gov.uk

>Index

buildings 13, 20

cab 8, 10, 28
cars 17
clothes 20, 27

emergencies 18, 25, 28
engine 10, 11
equipment 12, 16, 21, 22,
    27, 28

fire 7, 14, 17, 19, 20, 21,
    22, 25, 29
fire station 9, 23

hoses 14, 15, 22, 28

ladders 13, 26, 28
levers 8
lights 13, 19, 28
lockers 15, 16, 22, 28, 29

pedals 8
PPV unit 17

radio 9, 29

sirens 13, 19
steering wheel 8

tools 17, 29
tyres 11

water pump 14
wheels 11, 28